CW01677214

# SAM BOURNE

## The Best Poacher in Sussex

Ken Bourne

KSB Resources and Publishing Company

FOREST GROVE, BC Canada

**KSB Resources and Publishing Company**
**4473 Eagle Creek Road**
**FOREST GROVE**
**BC V0K 1M0**
**Canada**



**SAM BOURNE- Author Ken Bourne**—1st Edition-2017
ISBN 978-0-9958805-0-4

This book is dedicated to my grandfather,
Sam Bourne

*ABSQUE LABORE NIHIL*

My School Motto

(Without Work Nothing)

Brighton Hove and Sussex Grammar School

# CONTENTS

Chapter 1

# SAM BOURNE

## A Victorian adjusting to the 20th Century

Decades before the death of Queen Victoria, my grandfather grew up during the industrial revolution. He learned to drive steam tractors on the farm and witnessed the inventions of cars, planes, electricity, phones and machines that replaced workers in many industries. He married one of the Mitchell sisters from Cuckfield and fathered 12 children. When he got married, he and his family originally lived in Cuckfield, but later moved to Queen's Road, Haywards Heath, and then to Kents Road, also in Haywards Heath.

Obviously raising that many children in the first part of the twentieth century was an enormous task for a labourer, but he and my grandmother were up to the task. She cleaned other people's houses and took in laundry. Granddad was a charcoal burner.

He also operated several coppices, grew a large garden and supplemented the family meals with pheasants, rabbits, pigeons and ducks from some of the surrounding farms and estates. Most of the time, this was without the knowledge or consent of the owners.

Yes! He was a poacher! Granddad had the reputation of being the best in the area, and provided many of his neighbours with their Sunday dinner. Poaching in the early years of the 20th century was a necessity for the working class as the cost of beef was beyond many families. Poaching was also frowned on by the owners of the larger estates, as they used the weekends and the land occupied by their tenants for shooting parties with their rich friends.

Rabbits and pigeons were very abundant but tenant farmers were not allowed to hunt them as their tenancy agreements forbade them from reducing these pests, or even having any for their own table. They often turned a blind eye to the odd poacher taking some! Earning a living wage for most people meant hard work and lots of it! Granddad worked hard, but had lots of fun too.

He enjoyed a pint of stout at the local pub, as well as darts, drafts and crib, and racing his whippet hounds. In his younger days he was a steam tractor driver on a farm, and when I knew him, which was just after the second World War, he was a charcoal burner on a local estate and had the lease on several coppices in Balcombe, Cuckfield, Lindfield, Walstead, and Wivelsfield.

He rode to work on his Raleigh bicycle, which he cared for carefully.(I was sometimes given the honour of cleaning and oiling it!)

This is a photo of the exact advertisement in the Smallholder magazine from which he bought his Raleigh. I still have many of these magazines, which he used to keep in one of the cupboards next to the fireplace in the sitting room.

My first memories of my grandparents go back to when I was 3 or 4 years old. My parents and I would walk from our Bentswood Crescent home to visit Granddad Sam and Grandma at Kents Road, and we were never the only visitors. Often it would be one of my many uncles and their family or a neighbour who had just popped in for a cup of tea, or a glass of Granddad's very potent homemade wine! When my dad was a teenager he and two of his brothers decided to sample some dandelion wine they had found in granddad's shed.

Grandma found them asleep several hours later. When they woke up they not only had an awful hangover headache but a very sore butt caused by granddad's leather belt!

On our visits, which were at least weekly, my favourite pastime was to get in the pen with granddad's whippets and 'help' them eat their dog biscuits. Granddad used to give them pieces of charcoal, which he said was the reason they won so many races. I liked the charcoal too and there are lots of family stories of me with black lips and face, having a great time as the dogs licked me clean!

Every time I arrived at my grandparent's house Granddad always said, "I am so glad you came, Kenny. I really need your help." I felt so proud and did anything that granddad asked. In fact it was me that benefited from his requests as most of the things I was asked to do were fun. I was very proud of my granddad. He was my hero. He taught me a lot and I am very grateful that I knew him, if only for a few years.

My granddad died when I was eleven but he was able to congratulate me when I got a scholarship to Brighton Grammar School. I still remember many of the incidents even though they happened nearly 60 years ago. He was very particular about many things and I always wondered how Grandma put up with his quirks. (Some people who know me say that I have inherited some of them!) I know they both loved each other very much and they shared that love with all of the family.

Granddad smoked cigarettes and a pipe. He always had a special armchair next to the fire in the dining room. He tended the fire and made sure that the kettle that was always on the hob was full of water that was hot enough to make the tea. The teapot was never cleaned. It was just rinsed, as cleaning it would spoil the taste of the tea. He wore black leather work boots and religiously polished them as he sat by the fire every evening after dinner.

He hated swearing! I found that out when I tried to use a 'grown-up's word that I had heard. My mouth was washed out with carbolic soap. Never did that again, at least not where granddad could hear me.

Although Grandma had very painful feet due to her diabetes, she took in washing and appeared, to me, to be always using the gas boiler or hanging up clothes, ironing or cooking. She was constantly working. But never without a smile! For Grandma, who had 12 children, I think life must have been very difficult. This is my grandparents at their house in Kents Road, Haywards Heath.

Many illnesses and children's diseases were often treated with home remedies. Honey and lemon was for colds. Syrup of figs was for regularity. Cod Liver Oil was for our daily vitamins and Castor Oil to cure constipation. The last mentioned medicine worked very quickly, often in the middle of the night, with disastrous results! Most 'cures' tasted so awful, that kids had to be very ill to complain enough to get the medicine! My father had his tonsils taken out on the kitchen table. One of his brothers had a broken arm set and put in splints without any anesthetic. Another brother had his broken ribs bound up with tight bandages and these were not taken off until his chest hairs grew through them! He said that when the nurse took off the bandages that it was more painful than when he broke his ribs.

The following stories about Sam Bourne are all true and I think that you will agree with me that without a doubt he was the best poacher in Sussex.

CHAPTER THREE

# WHIPPETS

Granddad loved his Whippets, although he would never admit it. One day I was playing with some toy lead soldiers behind his shed and I heard him talking to the dogs in their pen. He said, "It is time to go out for a run, my beauties. Here's a little something special for you. You run well this afternoon and I will give you some more." I popped my head round the corner and said, "Who are you talking to granddad?" He looked a little startled and said in his gruffest voice," These stupid dogs- you have to tell them who the boss is you know!" In his hand he had a couple of grandma's special oatmeal biscuits.

If she knew she would have made his life hell as she made them especially for the crib nights with her friends. He looked at me and held a finger to his lips, smiled and gave me one and ate the other biscuit himself. "I guess I will have to take you to the races today". That was a treat I was looking forward to. I had never been to the races as granddad always said I was too young.

The 'Races' were a Sunday afternoon ritual that got granddad all dressed up in his suit and highly polished boots. The whippets were brushed and had a leather lead each and were jumping straight up in the air with excitement, until granddad put their leads on. From then on they were on their best behaviour. The whippet races were held in a field at the rear of the local mental asylum, St. Francis Hospital. The hospital owned the farm and several of Granddads friends owned whippets and they competed against each other every weekend in the summer.

## Lookout for the local copper!

This was a serious affair. It was also an event for men only. Granddad and I and two of my uncles walked up the twitten at the top of Kents Road, took a roundabout route to the field, and everyone helped to set up the course. I was given the responsible job as lookout for the local bobby. I had to watch the road near the only entrance and tell granddad if I saw the local Constable coming on his bike. (All the times I went to the races I never saw him.)

## The Race

All of the whippets wore muzzles at the races. This was to stop them biting each other during the race and after each race so that they could not destroy the lure, which was a bundle of rabbit furs and bright rags. The lure was pulled along the course attached to a motor bike that was always ridden by an ex-army dispatch rider. I loved the motor bike and was always given a ride after the races.. The rope that pulled the lure was attached to the doors of the little boxes that held the dogs at the start of the race. The motor bike would start with a roar and pulled the lure in front of the boxes across an area that had been whitened with powdered chalk.

The doors of the boxes would burst open and the whippets burst out and started to chase what they imagined was a rabbit. The course was about 220 yards long for the adult dogs and a shorter distance for the puppies. The racing puppies were not small at all and looked the same as the other dogs, to me. At the end of the race the rider would stop and the dogs were all collected. Before the start of each race each owner would put a shilling in the pot (a jam jar) and the winner would take it all, normally six- shillings. That was good money then. There was some betting on the outcome by the spectators and that was the reason we kept a lookout for the police. At the end I was paid a half-penny by each of the dog owners. That was three-pence, a whole lot of sweets then and enough to buy some extra marbles. Granddad used to breed his whippets and I believe he sold the puppies and made extra money that way. His dogs won most of the races so his puppies were always in demand.

## The famous Tea Caddy

When we got back home, after the races, grandma was always there, waiting, with some orange juice for me, and a cup of tea for granddad. Her first words were, "How many races did you win?" Whatever the result granddad would always give her two half crowns (five shillings) and grandma would open the cupboard above his chair and take out an old tea-caddy. It always seemed heavy and she put the two half crowns in it. This was the special tin. It was opened on the grandchildren's birthdays and the appropriate one was given a half crown to put in a post office savings account. It was also used for other special occasions such as Christmas and Easter. Grandma had other 'banks' as well, one for the farthings and half-pennies they used in the games of crib, and another for the silver three-penny pieces she always put in the Christmas pudding. This was later increased to sixpence!

## The real whippet races.

The whippets had other uses than just winning races. They chased and caught rabbits. This was my favourite pastime, but I was only able to go with granddad a few times a year. Grandma would pack us both a lunch and granddad would have his beer bottle filled with cold tea. Then with one dog on a lead and granddad pushing his trusty Raleigh bike, we would head off for the long walk to the fields behind the hospital or even to Ditchling Common. One of the destinations I loved was the fields around Folly Farm, in Rocky Lane. Some fields bordered the railway and I could look over the fence and wave to the steam-train driver. He always waved back and pulled the chain that made the train whistle to me,"Whoo, whoo!" Unfortunately the railway bridge there got a sad reputation. Sometimes a patient from St. Francis Hospital would fall over the wall onto the line. (They actually committed suicide!) These deaths eventually resulted in a wire barrier being put up.

When we got to our destination granddad would park his bike and release the dog to have a run. Then we were ready for the serious job of getting rabbits. No talking and tread quietly! The dog would run ahead a few yards sniffing and granddad would signal by a series of whistles. One for go right, two for go left and a long one to make the dog lie down. He obeyed every command, not because he was afraid, but because the hunt was so much fun. Ears alert and noses held high he would find any rabbit that was nearby. If he missed one granddad would see it and direct the dog to its hiding place.

Once found the rabbit would run towards its burrow following a path that had been there for generations of rabbits. The whippet was always quicker and when it caught the rabbit it would grab it by the neck and flip it backwards, immediately breaking its neck. Granddad would whistle the dog to lie down and go and get the rabbit. The next event took me a little time to get used to. Granddad would immediately gut the rabbit with his pocket knife and give the dog the heart and liver. As it was eating them the dog would growl and look from side to side. Granddad warned me not to go near the dog as it would definitely bite me if I did. That is one warning that I heeded! He would slice one of the back legs of the rabbit and made a hole, through which he pushed the other leg. He then hung the rabbit on the handlebars of his bike.

Sometimes we never saw a rabbit but other times we were very lucky and came home with sometimes as many as six rabbits hanging on the handlebars. We kept some for ourselves and often gave one to a neighbour. When he had enough, granddad would take them to the local butcher. Getting rabbits from the Common was legal, as was hunting them on private land with permission. Once they were on the handlebars and we were walking along the road nobody knew where they came from. That made it very exciting!

# Hunting rats.

The whippets had even another use, and that was even more exciting, and even greater fun. Sometimes granddad and a group of his friends would go to the Hospital farm barn to hunt for rats. They all had baler twine tied around the bottom of their trouser legs, in case a rat ran up their leg! I only wore shorts that came down to my knees but had to have them tied up too. The barn contained some bags of oats to feed the farm animals but the rats had found them first.

The hunt was on to find their nests and to get rid of them. Rats like to build their nests in dark places, so under the hay bales was the first place to search. Armed with shovels, granddad and friends carefully lifted each bale with a pitch fork and soon found a nest with young rats. Immediately the rats were running everywhere. The men chased them all over the barn with shovels clanging and hob nailed boots thumping as they tried to stamp on the rodents. They got a few but the whippets were quicker and caught the rest.

No more nests were found but there were still some adult rats that were heard scratching and squeaking in the oats at the bottom of a damaged sack. The oats were tipped out and this time the men did not use their shovels to attack the rats but to defend themselves from the rats. The whippets were not scared, they went right in with a snap, snap, snap and that was the end of that excitement. The farm foreman was very grateful and we all went to his house for refreshments. This was homemade cider in a very large five-gallon glass jar. I was allowed a sip but it tasted so sour to me that I spat it out. The foreman's wife gave the men a tongue wagging for giving me the cider and she gave me some lemonade and chocolate biscuits instead. I liked her! By the way, I love cider now. However, here in Canada we can't get my favourites, Scrumpy or Merrydown.

Chapter 3

# THE CATAPULT

## A silent killer in expert hands!

The catapult, or slingshot, is often thought of as a kids' toy. That is so far from the truth! In the right hands it is a deadly weapon and can kill a rabbit up to 50 feet away. Granddad was an expert. He made his own catapults and used them to hunt rabbits, pheasants, ducks and pigeons, and if a farmer paid him he would shoot crows that were nesting near crops. He could also destroy their nests and eggs with a few well-aimed shots. They were much cheaper to use that shot-guns and much quieter too. In the depression and up to the Second World War, granddad made extra money by shooting grey squirrels and getting a bounty of 2 and a half pence per tail. The current wage for a labourer then was about 30 shillings a week, or six pence an hour! He used to attract a squirrel by making a squeaking sound by sucking on the skin between his thumb and first finger. He said it sounded like another squirrel invading his territory, so it came down the tree to investigate. That was a huge mistake and the last one the squirrel would make!

He taught me how to make and use a catapult, and I eventually became quite a good shot. One of the drawers next to his chair by the fire was filled with catty strods that were in various stages of aging and hardening before he made them into catapults. The strods were 'Y' shaped branches of hazel, chestnut or hawthorn trees that granddad was always on the lookout for when he was making charcoal in the woods. I prefer willow as that wood is easily shaped and stays that way after a few weeks. He would put them in the drawer for a year, and when they were hardened enough he would use them to make catapults for himself, or swap them in the pub for a pint of stout.

This photo is of some "strods" that I have that are being hardened for later use.

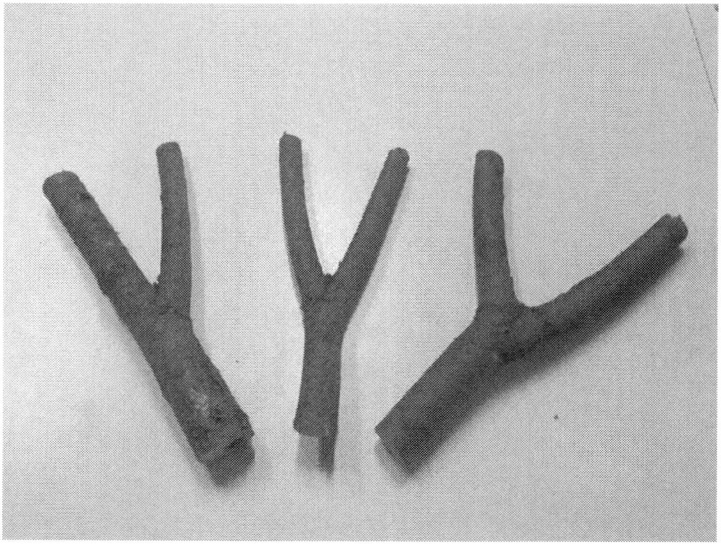

The other two drawers next to his chair had some special treasures that I inherited when he died. One drawer was full of cigarette cards that granddad had collected over many decades, with beautiful pictures of soldiers uniforms, birds, flowers, butterflies and almost every other subject imaginable. The other had hundreds of lead soldiers, lead musket balls which granddad made from a musket-ball maker (it looked like an old pair of pliers with a hole in it). He used these balls in his catapult.

Also in the drawer was a collection of stone-age tools and weapons that he had found when he was digging trenches for the houses being built in Boltro Road, Haywards Heath. Somehow these artifacts vanished when he died. I didn't have much luck with the cigarette card or soldiers either. My step-sisters took them to school and swapped them for dollies! I still have the musketball maker though, and some of his catapult strods. I also was lucky enough to find his bill-hook, years later, which he had used in the woods to cut bean poles and other branches from the trees in his coppices. I still use it. This is his billhook!

## Making the catapults.

The catapult was such an important tool that granddad took the utmost care when he made a new one. They were made from three items that were chosen very carefully. The first was the strod. This had to be the right diameter and shape, and come from wood that would harden over time. His favourite wood was chestnut, but he used hazel, silver birch and yew when he could get it. He always said that archers used yew for their bows so it should be even better for catapults.

The next item was the rubber that was attached to each side of the strod. Granddad did this by making a hole through the top of each side of the strod. He would heat up a nail on the gas stove until it was red hot and then, holding it with a pair of pliers, push it through the wood. The rubber had to be strong and not have any weak parts, because if it broke it could easily spring back and damage your eye. He used the rubber from discarded car inner tubes and would go to the local garage and trade a rabbit for a few. My first catapults were made from these and worked great. Granddad used wider strips for his and I could not pull them back at all. I guess that is why he was able to shoot a rabbit from so far away. When the square rubber was introduced especially for catapults, he reluctantly tried it and found that it really was better.

The pouch that held the ammunition when he made a shot (lead balls that he made, or sometimes round stones or even marbles) was also important. It had to be leather and soft enough to cling to the ammunition but strong enough not to snap under pressure. He used the leather tongue from old work boots. With the rest of the boot he would make leather laces, muzzles for the whippets and even elbow patches for his coat. Not much was wasted in his house.

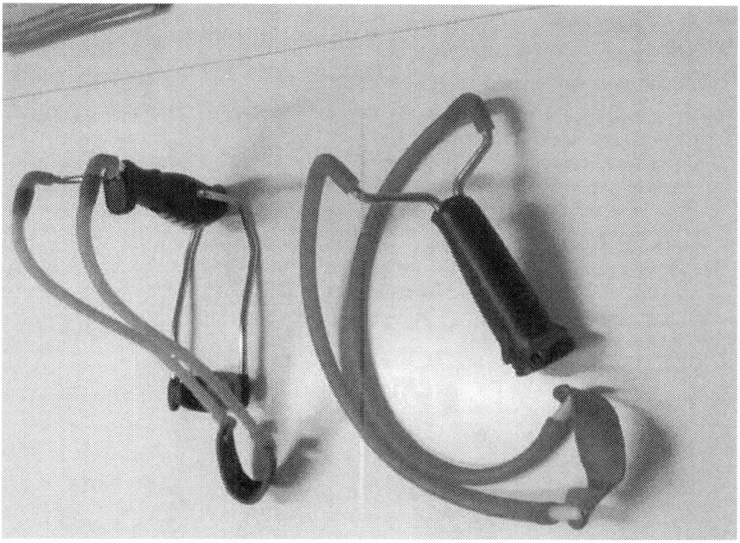

## Charlie the boot repairer.

My grandfather used to put the hob-nails in his own boots and those of the rest of the family. But when he needed new soles it was my job to take the boots to Charlie, the shoe repairer who operated behind Russell's Sweet Shop in New England Road. Charlie was a dwarf and did a very good job repairing all sorts of footwear. He was also the brunt of many jokes aimed at him from the local kids. I was always a bit scared of him but he was always nice to everyone. I would take granddad's boots together with a rabbit to Charlie and without being asked he would give me some old leather boots and even some leather pieces that were too small for him to use.

Granddad often practiced with the catapults and taught me how to shoot accurately. Just above his house there was a piece of unused land that had an old gatepost in the middle. The top of the post was flat and he would take his jack knife, stab it in the top and put a silver three-penny bit in the slot. This was a special coin that had a small hole near the edge. Threaded through the hole was about a yard of bright red silk yarn. This made it easy for me to find it when granddad hit the coin. He would pace off 50 feet, take aim and fire. He never missed. The coin would be propelled a long way and it was my job to retrieve it. No wonder he got so many rabbits, pigeons, ducks and pheasants

Chapter 4

# CHARCOAL

## The ancient art reincarnated

Making charcoal was a dirty, 24 hour job, that took several days to complete and granddad was away from home for over a week. The process was and is still an art, but back then it was really hard work. Everything was done by hand. The trees were felled with a crosscut saw and an axe. The larger ones were pulled to the kiln by a team of draft horses.

Then the trees were bucked into 4 foot lengths and piled into a cord. A cord is a pile of wood 4 feet wide, 8 feet long and 4 feet high. When the pile was as large as he wanted,( this was often several cords) granddad would then cover it completely with turves, or sod, so that the pile was completely airtight. This was to stop oxygen from coming into the pile after the fire was lit. One turf on the top and one right at the bottom was removed and the fire was lit from the bottom. The hole at the top served as a chimney. The bottom one was the damper, which controlled the draft to get the fire red hot. The next process was critical as one mistake meant starting all over again.

The fire had to burn extremely hot at the bottom so that the heat from the embers would start to sear the wood above. At this stage the top and bottom turves were replaced so that the fire was deprived of oxygen and the wood would still burn but not turn to ashes. Depending on the size of the pile the process could take up 4 days to turn the wood into charcoal. Granddad only took a nap for an hour or less, in his camp, which was a tarpaulin stretched over a sapling leaning up against a larger tree.

The estate foreman would supply granddad with cold tea and a ploughman's lunch, which was a hunk of cheese, an onion and a slice of homemade bread. His wife often added some buttered scones as a treat.

Each pile of cordwood had to be made from the same species of wood. Oak was the most often used as the trunk would be used from lumber and the branches for fencing or charcoal. Ash and beech was also used, but apparently the best and most expensive charcoal was made from birch. Granddad preferred the birch as it was cleaner, smaller and much easier to process than the other varieties.

## Granddad's 'secret' garden additive-Biochar.

He used to bring a bag of birch charcoal home for his dogs and used to put some on his garden. He was way ahead of his time! He had, like most gardeners, a compost heap. One day his bag of charcoal was leaning against the compost when it rained. The rain soaked the compost and the juices in it leaked onto the bag. He could not use the charcoal so he just tipped it onto his garden. He planted cabbages where the charcoal had been put and had the biggest and tastiest crop ever. So he brought home more every spring and mixed it with a 'tea' he made from his compost. This tea he fed to his vegetables and he had very constant, impressive results. "They like tea as much as I do!" he would say.

He didn't know it, but he was doing exactly what the Amazonian people did to feed their huge population over a thousand years ago. They put trees in a trench and burned them. They then covered the trees with soil and the result was charcoal. As they grew organically, the charcoal turned the soil black and kept it fertile. Their soil is still fertile and now has the name 'terra preta' which is Portuguese for dark earth.

The bonus of this procedure is that it stores carbon in the soil and reduces the amount of greenhouse gases in the atmosphere. In fact I took up horticulture as a career and now I write about organic gardening and my pet subject is Bio-char, the modern name for charcoal used in growing food crops. I make my own bio-char for the plants and vegetables in my organic nursery. I hope I can make a difference in someone's life the same as my granddad did!

The fires he made produced more than charcoal. Often granddad would take some old wine bottles with him. These would be filled with wet clay and placed in the hot kiln. When the fire eventually cooled down and the results were amazing! The bottles would be twisted and the glass distorted by the heat. The clay stopped the glass from melting or breaking, and the colours were changed so that they reflected light like a diamond. These bottles were then washed and sold to a local electrician who turned them into very nice table lamps.

This man, I think his name was Mister Anderson, lived in Bentswood Road and also charged up the accumulators that powered the radios to which most people listened to the news.

I loved to listen to the radio series about a 'Mountie' in Canada. It was called "Sergeant Preston of the Yukon". Funny that is where I now live! A little further south than the Yukon though..

Chapter 5

# FERRETS

## Unusual pets today- but deadly hunters!

Whippets were not the only animals that granddad used to help him get enough food to feed his family. He also had several ferrets that he kept in a cage outside his garden shed. I did not like them! They had sharp teeth and one bit my finger when I poked it through the netting of the cage. My fault, but it hurt and I had to go the hospital for an injection against tetanus (we called it lockjaw then).

These were definitely not pets. They did a job. They killed rabbits very efficiently and also chased them out of their burrows. This was also a death sentence as when the rabbit burst out of the hole it was entangled in the net that had been strategically placed over the exit.

Granddad's overcoat pockets were the home for the ferrets when he went to get rabbits at places where he did not have permission. No policeman or gamekeeper would bother to put their hands in to check to find out if he had any with him! Many rabbit burrows were in the bank alongside the hedge that was on the boundary of these estates, so sometimes he didn't have to trespass to get a few rabbits.

However most of the times he used ferrets was when the owner of a smaller farm was overrun with rabbits and asked granddad to help. Granddad and a couple of his friends would meet at the home of the rabbits whose burgeoning population had offended their landlord. The Raleigh bike was loaded up as usual. This time it was loaded with a sack of ferrets and several nets.

Setting up the nets was a very strategic operation, and everyone knew their job. The rabbit burrow has several entrances and exits and the rabbits used these to try to make their escape. Great care was taken to put a net over every bolt hole. The nets were called purse nets because when a rabbit hit it the string around the top tightened just like a purse, trapping the rabbit inside. Each net was spread carefully over the hole and the string that was wound around the edge had to be at the top. This was to ensure that the loop in the string could easily slide and close the net. The string was attached to a metal stake that was pushed into the ground. Not hammered in like a tent peg, as this would frighten the rabbits.

The men would then stop for a quick cigarette. Discuss the strategy and then get down to the serious business of thinning out this warren. Two ferrets were put in different holes from one side and the men then waited near the holes on the opposite side of the warren. Soon one would put up a hand. They did not speak as it was imperative there was no noise. This man had heard some scratching noises. A rabbit was being chased and would soon explode out of the hole.

Wham! A rabbit ran straight into a net and was trapped, struggling to get out. The nearest man had to be very quick.

He would open the net, grab the rabbit and quickly dispatch it by holding the back legs in one hand and the head in the other. A twist of the wrist and it was all over. The net was put back and the hunt continued. Sometimes a rabbit escaped, which caused some swearing, but granddad always said," Leave it we must leave some to make more rabbits for next year." He was right! By leaving a few that meant that the warren would soon be replenished and the farmer would ask for their services the following year. In the end there were no more noises heard and the ferrets would pop their heads out of the hole. They would be given a reward for their work, the same as the whippets. This was a piece of liver or kidney after the rabbits had been gutted.

Sometimes a ferret would not appear. This meant that it had caught a rabbit and was enjoying a meal down the hole. This was a huge problem, as the wayward animal would have to be dug out. Some people would put a collar on the ferret and a long string so they could be pulled out if necessary. Granddad did not do this, as he preferred his ferrets to come out for their special treat.

When the hunt was over the farmer would take a few rabbits for himself, and the rest were shared out between the men. This was not work for them and they could exchange their excess rabbits for pints of beer or stout at the local pub!

Chapter 6

# SNARES

## Think like a rabbit- or you will not catch any.

There is an art in setting a snare to trap a rabbit. They are creatures of habit and if you don't understand their habits then you will be disappointed with your efforts. Granddad did not kill animals for sport. He did so because he had to feed his family. He believed that wild animals could not be owned by anybody.

When he did kill them he did so humanely and as quickly as possible.

When I was in my pre-teen years hunting and trapping was very exciting to me. Today I have different opinions, but would hunt and trap if my family needed feeding and there was no other way.

Here in Canada hunting is thought of by many as a right and many animals are killed just for fun or for trophies, and the meat left to rot. I totally disagree with that, as the number of wild animals has been drastically reduced.

Granddad taught me lot about wildlife, plants, trees, and many of the old crafts. I am really grateful for that.

## Setting Snares

Rabbits in England live mostly in burrows, warrens, or sets. Basically these are a series of holes or tunnels that are often inter-connected, and on a higher level than the rest of the land. I believe this is to avoid flooding.

When the rabbits leave their home they always travel on the same path. There are many paths around each warren and every rabbit will use them. When you approach a warren you can easily see these paths. They are well worn with the grass or soil flattened down at regular intervals. This is because the rabbit travels in a series of jumps. Every rabbit will follow the path and jump in the same place as other rabbits. Knowing these habits and reading the paths is the way that hunters are able to trap the rabbits. The snare is a loop of wire attached to a stake. The snare is set up along the path and the rabbit will because of its habit, put its head in the noose, with deadly consequences.

It is the strategic placing of the noose that determines the success of the hunter. As a rabbit hops along the path from each jump to the next, he has his ears up. To ensure the rabbit's head goes through the noose without restriction it should be about 6 inches in diameter. The placing of the snare is also critically important. There are two types of flattened down areas in the path. Most are narrow and small in diameter. These are the jumping points along the path. The other areas are wider and longer, and often have some rabbit poop on them. Those areas are where the rabbit lays down.

You must find a series of the narrow jumps and set the noose of the snare exactly in the middle of one. The height of the bottom of the snare should be about six and a half inches from the ground, and is normally held there by a small forked stick or a piece of stiff wire. Granddad used to measure this distance by making a fist with his thumb sticking up.

Adults used to use many body parts for measurements. The clenched fist was used to measure the height of horses, hence the term 'hands', which is 4 inches. The tip of the fingers to the elbow is about 18 inches. Elbow to wrist is about a foot. The measurement across the thumb just below the nail is an inch. I guess this is not very accurate as everyone is different! However, you only have to look at the human figure sketch by Leonardo da Vinci to begin to understand that the human proportions and mathematical calculations are all interrelated!

Setting the snares took granddad about four hours. He would take a circuitous route around the farm, and then have some lunch. He explained that after being disturbed, the rabbits needed some time to calm down and get back to eating and the other things that rabbits do. Also he did not want to leave any rabbits in the snares for too long, as the meat would spoil if they were not gutted. He would start at the beginning again and check each snare. Many would have caught a rabbit and some were not touched at all. He made sure that he collected all the snares and put them back in the sack.

Over the years the attitude towards hunting and killing defenseless animals has changed and so has mine. I do not hunt anymore although I still own and often carry a Lee Enfield 303 rifle around my property in Canada, as recently my wife was confronted by a cougar (mountain lion) which had just made a meal of one of our cats, in the hay barn.

Chapter 7

# FISHING

## Teach a young man to fish…give him a hobby for life.

Fishing is one aspect of hunting, that I have done legally, all my life, and I thank my grandfather and my father for introducing me to the art of angling. In the late 1940's and 1950's there were many places to fish that were free and easily accessible. At that time Ditchling Common pond was one of my favourites. However my first attempts at catching the elusive fish was in the little brook that runs under the bridge on the footpath between Washington Road, Haywards Heath and Lindfield Common.

The gudgeon was my prey. They were easily seen in the clear water of the brook, and looked as if they would be easy to catch. I never caught one, even though I offered them the tastiest pieces of bait that I could find. I made my own rods and fishing gear and I was so proud of my efforts.

My rod was a stout piece of bamboo. My line was a length of white needlework thread tied to the end of the rod and the other attached to the hook. The hook was a work of art in itself! I made mine out of a dressmaking pin that was bent at the sharp end using a pair of pliers. This was dangerous work as I often stuck the pin in my finger. My baits ranged from small pieces of cheese, a ball of dough made from flour and bread, and worms! I loved the worms as we had loads in my dad's garden and they were great fun to make the local girls scream!

Two of my teachers were the recipients of some of my biggest worms. A couple of school friends and I would keep a lookout and put them in the drawer of the teacher's desk at the then new school in New England Road. One teacher, a Mrs. Balls, used to ride her bicycle to school all the way from Burgess hill, rain or shine. The bag on her bike was often given a gift of some worms and even a frog found its way into the bag once. She never screamed. She carefully lifted it out and put it into the grass at the side of the bike rack. We admired her. She was tough! We were also a little scared of her.

Granddad had a real fishing rod. It was very long, to me, and made from split cane. It had three pieces that fitted together and gran had made him a canvas case for it. He also had a brass reel and proper fishing line and hooks. One day, I think I was about 6 years old, my father, granddad and I went on our first fishing trip together to Ditchling Common pond. My father had a van, which he used for his landscaping business. It was a Morris Commercial, built before the Second World War. Back then vehicles lasted for decades, if you looked after them. Plus they were easy to repair if they ever broke down, unlike the computer controlled vehicles of today!

## Murder at the Royal Oak

On the way, just past the Fox and Hounds pub, my dad and granddad would talk about the man who came to that pub and won lots of money playing darts with sharpened 6 inch nails. This is also the pub where my father's horse used to pull into the yard of his own accord as he always got a pint of beer with his hay as dad went in for his lunch. At the next pub, the Royal Oak, they pointed out the hanging tree where a murderer, Jacob Harris, was hung. They also showed me Jacob's Post.

This was erected in the late 1800's and was supposed to be at the place where the gallows were. But the local story is that he was executed in Horsham and his body brought back to the scene of his crime. He had slit the throat of owner of the Royal Oak pub, killed his wife and daughter, robbed the place and fled. His body was wrapped in chains and hung from the oak tree until his body rotted and then buried where the post is. Funny how kids love gory, bloodthirsty stories!

Just up the road from the pub were some old gateposts that held the tollgate to the common. Anyone who wanted to travel across the common had to pay a toll every time! Granddad also showed me a piece of wood that had been cut from the post and said that some gypsies had told him that it would stop toothaches. We all laughed because he had only a few onion chasers left!

## Ditchling Common Pond

We turned into Spatham Lane at the other end of the common and parked the van on the grass at the side of the road. It was only a short walk to the pond and it looked enormous to me. There was a huge area of water with a large area at the back of bull-rushes. At the end of the path along the bank, was a little bridge that went over the small stream that ran from the pond. Granddad said that this was the place for me to fish, as there were always lots of roach there.

They both set me up for my first attempt at 'real' fishing. I still had my rod, as I wanted it to catch my first fish on my own rod. A length of real fishing line was tied to the end of the rod and a real hook tied on the end of the line. I was given a float that was attached to the line with a small elastic band. The float was made from a feather with the end painted red with some of my sister's nail polish. Granddad measured the depth of the pond and made the line from the hook to the float a little longer than that. He then put a small lead weight on the line about 6 inches from the hook. I was shown how to put a piece of worm on the hook and then I was ready to go.

## My First Fish!

My first attempts were disastrous! The worm flew off the hook. The line tangled around the end of the rod and the hook caught in the branches of a small tree. Luckily both the men were patient with me and eventually I got the message. "Slow down! Do everything gently! Don't make so much noise! Let the float lie flat. The float is going under, wait, wait. Now steady, lift the rod and walk back a step. He's on! Pull it out! There! Your first fish! What a whopper! It must be at least 6 inches- biggest roach I have ever seen!" At these words I was the proudest boy in Sussex. No, in the World!

However, that exhilaration was short-lived. Granddad wanted to fish for pike, and needed a fish for live bait. My poor little roach fitted the bill exactly. I really wanted to take my first fish home to show mum. But I was persuaded to give up the fish in return for a promise of a real fishing rod that granddad had been keeping for my next birthday. So the roach had a big hook through its upper lip, and another through its dorsal fin. These hooks had thin wire attached to them as pike have very sharp teeth that can bite through normal fishing line (or fingers if they get in the way!). The line had a large cork float about 2 feet away from the fish, which allowed it to swim around.

To put the float and the fish in the right area to attract the pike granddad got me to go the other of end of the pond with him. He then put the float and fish in the water and gave me a loop of line to hold while he went round the pond to the other side letting the line off of his fishing reel as he went. When he got to the other side he called for me to let go of the line. He then started to slowly pull the float across the pond. He would pull in about 15 feet of line and then stop for a while. He continued doing this until the float reached the middle of the pond about 10 feet from the bull rushes. He left it there for some time and the float started to move around in small circles.

## The Pike, a dangerous predator!

Granddad said quietly, "A pike is there and your roach is trying to get away." Right at that moment there was an enormous splash and the float started moving very fast towards the bulrushes. Granddad reached down and grabbed the rod and pulled it up and backwards holding the reel so that no more line came off. "Got him!" he said, and his face lit up with the biggest smile I have ever seen. He started to reel in the line and tried to steer the pike away from the bulrushes. After what seemed an eternity he got the pike close to the shore and said to Dad, "Sid pick up the gaff." Dad reached down and got hold of a broom handle with a large, sharp metal hook on the end. The pike was splashing in the shallow water in front of us and Dad stretch out and hooked the pike under the lower jaw and pulled him out onto the grass bank.

To me, that pike looked enormous.( At home he weighed almost 10 pounds.) Granddad had his fish-bonker, which was a piece of old hosepipe with some lead in one end. He hit the pike just behind its head and it just shook for a few seconds and then stopped. "He looks like he's dead, but keep your fingers away from his mouth as they sometimes bite when you think they are finished." Dad said. As granddad was taking his fishing hook out of the pike's mouth, he burst out laughing as he pulled out my roach which was still alive. I was really happy as I was able to take it home so that I could show my first fish to Mum. My mother cooked my roach and grandma cooked the big pike. I tasted both and to me they tasted awful. They also had lots of bones that got caught in my throat and made me want to be sick. It was a long time before I would eat any fish again! This did not affect my love for actually trying to catch them. I used to go fishing as often as I could. I had to persuade an adult to take me as I could not swim then.

My father and granddad showed me several new places to fish that were fairly close to home. The nearest one was the brook between Hanbury Lane, Haywards Heath, and Lindfield Common.

You could actually see the fish in the brook, there were minnows and gudgeon. I never caught any with my fishing rod, but I did get minnows in a butterfly net.

## Harlands Pit

The best fishing pond, at that time was Harland's Pit, a private pond at the top of Lucastes Avenue. It had lots of different fish in it. These included, Roach, Perch, Tench, Carp and Pike. A few of the pike and carp were very big. I heard of some people who had caught fish there that weighed more than 20 pounds!

The family who owned the property were very nice people who would give local anglers permission to fish in Harlands Pit. They had rules that nearly everyone obeyed; no rubbish, no damage, no noise and every fish caught had to be returned to the pond. If you were lucky enough to catch a large one, they would take a photo of the fish, and weigh it. They would then put the photo on their garden shed door and give a copy to the lucky angler. Over the years I caught lots of fish at Harland's Pit and am very grateful to the owners for allowing me to fish there.

## River Ouse- Lindfield

Lindfield is probably the most picturesque village in Sussex and has a fantastic history. , I used various methods of transportation to get to the River Ouse which is about a mile north of the village. When I went there with my mother or father we would go by bus which only took about 20 minutes.

There was a bus stop close to the bridge over the river. A short walk took us to a style which gave us access to the banks of the slow moving Ouse. On the left hand side of the river we would walk along the bank to the first hedge and fence. We had to climb over the fence into the next field.

At this point the river widened out considerably and this was where the local kids would come to swim. There was a diving board and the river was shallow enough to wade in at the edge. When no one was swimming this spot was favourite place to fish. Well it was until a disaster happened to me. I was fishing close the bank on the other side of the river with a worm on my hook for bait, when a group of Chinese ducks came paddling by. One dived under the water close to my float and gobbled up my worm. It then surfaced and started to flap its wings and tried to fly. This frightened me so much that I let go of my fishing rod and it fell into the water and was pulled behind the fleeing duck. That was the end of my day's fishing. On the way back to the road my mum saw the rod in the reeds close to the bank. The line had broken and the hook and float were missing. That day I learned to keep my bait away from ducks!

This fishing spot was a great place to go, and my friends and I would often ride our bicycles or even walk from Bentswood Crescent to the river. I learned to swim in that swimming area. There was an old raft tied to the diving board. The older boys had made it from a few steel barrels with planks of wood tied on the top of it. It floated, but was very hard to steer with 4 or 5 kids on it. Most of us learned to swim by being pushed off the raft into the river. Unfortunately a boy from Bentswood Crescent was drowned when he fell off the raft. This incident stopped those activities for a while but soon the raft was resurrected and a new group of daredevils continued with the tradition.

There were several other fishing spots that granddad showed me that were in cycling distance of Haywards Heath. Some were in the Cuckfield area where he lived for several years. Behind Cuckfield church there was a footpath that led down to a stream. At that point the owner of the land had built some small huts that were used as changing rooms. This was a really good place to fish and swim.

Coming out of Cuckfield, on the way to Ansty, there was a lake at Cuckfield Place. Lots of fish here!, There were some rumours of a giant catfish that was supposed to have been released into the lake when it became too large for the owners aquarium. Many anglers swore that they had hooked it but the fish was too strong for their fishing line and it got away.

On the road from Ansty to Hurstpierpoint (the lane that leads to the Sportsman Inn at Goddard's Green) there are two private lakes on the left side of the road. Both of these lakes hold large fish, but the second one has really huge pike. I was fishing there one day from the owner's rowing boat, and saw a huge pike swimming alongside the boat. The boat was about six feet long and the pike was nearly as long as the boat. I told the owner and he said they had often seen it before. One time he said they saw it attack and drag a duck under the water.

My favourite place to fish , especially when I was older, was Rushy Pit, a secluded pond at Paynes Place Farm. On the same farm there was stream that ran between the farm and West End Riding School, in Burgess Hill. Here I caught my first trout!

I am so grateful to my grandfather, for introducing me to the sport of fishing.

Chapter 8

# SUSSEX DIALECT

In the 1940s and 50's the Sussex Dialect was often heard spoken by the older generations. Often people who were born in Sussex stayed and worked in Sussex all their lives. In fact most people would live within 5 miles of where they were born. Consequently, local words and the method of pronouncing them would be passed from generation to generation. Anyone with a different accent would be classed as a foreigner Some people who started to move to Sussex for its convenient commuting distance and train service to London would often comment that the Sussex dialect was common. We thought Cockney was common! And we always thought that "posh" people spoke with a plum in their mouths.

Here are some of the words and phrases he used with the translation where needed.

"I be gonna teach you summat bout fishin." "Don't y tell no gurt fibs" ( Do not tell any big lies) " Y dursn't do that"(You should not do that) "Don'worry they durdledores dunna sting."(Don't worry those bumble bees do not sting) "All things in Sussex be a she, bar they Tom Cats, and they be a he" (No translation needed). "He wersent late surelye?"(Surely he was not late) He would pronounce violet as "voylet" and Chrysanthemum as "Christyanthem", Pony as "Po er-nee" Mice as "meeces" and Morning as "marnin". He often said to me, "Don't y be addle headed" (Do not be stupid) "Dinna argify with I" (Do not argue with me) "He be abeatin the Devil round the gooseberry bush" (He is taking a long time to get to the point of a story.)

I have not been back to Sussex for thirty years and I fear that few people there now speak with a Sussex accent or have even heard it.

Chapter 9

# GHOSTS AND SMUGGLERS

Sussex has an exciting history and there abounds many stories of intrigue. Some are true and some, probably most, are fiction, or have been enhanced by the storyteller's imagination.

Granddad was an excellent storyteller and often told me and some of my friends, thrilling stories of ghosts, strange happenings, and sometimes true stories of smugglers.

Lindfield

A few miles from Haywards Heath is the beautiful and historic village of Lindfield. I know the village very well as I once had a milk-round there. There are many fantastic very old houses throughout the village that are a legend in themselves.

Granddad's favourite story of Lindfield was about the smugglers who came through the village at night, with over 300 pack horses, that used to carry tea and other smuggled goods to London. These smugglers belonged to a very ruthless gang that tortured and murdered anyone who reported them to the Customs Officers. Even the Customs Officers were afraid of them.

As a result whenever the villagers heard the hooves of the horses, they would draw their curtains and extinguish any lights. This meant that the smugglers would leave the village in peace.

There was more smuggling activities that went on in the village itself. These were mostly centred in the area of the Church. The church at Lindfield is at the top of the hill just past the Bent Arms public house. Some of the oldest houses are there including Lindfield Place which was a hunting lodge of King Henry V111.

Past Lindfield Place and down the hill towards Ardingly is the River Ouse. This river was navigable two and a half centuries ago, all the way from Newhaven to at least the point where the present bridge crosses the Ouse at the bottom of this hill. Smugglers would collect their goods from ships in the English Channel and transport them by river to drop off places inland. One important drop off point was here at Lindfield.

There have always been rumours that tunnels were built from the river to some of the houses and other buildings in Lindfield. One day granddad took me fishing in the River Ouse. He showed me where one of the tunnels was. We were fishing near the left side of the road on the bank of the river closest to Lindfield. Granddad took me across the field towards Lindfield to a small hill just below a tall hedge. The hill was covered with grass. It was a mound really, not a hill, but to me it was big. He cut out a piece of turf from this mound and underneath it was part of a door in a brick wall. This was the entrance to one of the famous tunnels. He said the smugglers would bring the goods by river, unload them onto the bank. The owner of the house to where the tunnel leads would then take them either to the basement of the house or to the stables.

Years later I was doing some landscaping at this very house and asked the owner about the tunnel. The owner herself was quite old and lived there with her daughter.

She said that she had not seen the tunnel but understood that it had been filled in at the point where it entered the old stables.

An old gardener that I knew said the entrance to the tunnels was in the basement of the house and had been hidden by bricks.

The rumours say that there were also tunnels that led to Lindfield Place and even to the church or to the old Tiger Inn. There is a very old water mill below Lindfield place which would have been a good drop off point too.

There was an antique shop on the corner of the first road on the right just above the lovely Lindfield pond. On the wall outside there was huge metal man trap.

There were rumours that it had been made at the old blacksmith's shop which was nearby, and that smugglers had put these traps in the tunnels to scare off any intruders.

I used to watch the blacksmith who worked there when he was shoeing the carthorses that delivered the wood and coal at that time. He even let me help sometimes.

I had to pass him nails as he said he could no longer hold them in his teeth because a horse had kicked him in the face and he had none left.

When I got older and had my own horsesI learned to shoe horses and used the knowledge I had to demonstrate blacksmithing at a heritage ranch in British Columbia.

# Cuckfield

This is another old and beautiful village just to the west of Haywards Heath that also has a myriad of ghost and scary stories.

## The haunting of Cuckfield Place.

My most popular one was granddad telling the story of the local haunted house, Cuckfield Place.

Apparently the owner in the 1800's had a lengthy court battle with the then present owner, who had got possession of the manor house by false pretences. When she won the court battle, Dame Sergison, as she was called, ruled the estate with an iron hand and treated the staff and tenants abysmally. When she died few people were sad. However she reappeared on the scene when her granddaughter got married at Cuckfield Place.

After that it was regularly reported that on Christmas Eve it was impossible to light a fire in her old bedroom. Some people said she was often seen swinging on the iron gateway at the entrance to the state.

## Voices on a foggy evening.

My grandmother and her sister, my great aunt Amy, lived their early lives in Cuckfield. One foggy evening, (and back then in the early 1900's foggy meant almost pitch black,) they were both walking home from the church. They heard footsteps behind them, getting closer and closer. When these footsteps came really close a man's voice said" This is a very foggy night isn't it?" The two girls did not answer. Seconds later they came across a gas lamp that showed the whole road in front of them and behind. The sound of the footsteps had stopped but there was no sign of the person who had spoken to them. Luckily they were close to their family house so they ran home as fast as they could.

Chapter 10

# COUNTRYSIDE LORE

Living and working on farms and country estates all his life, my grandfather learned a lot about the lives of animals, birds, fish and plants. He tried to pass as much of this knowledge on to me as he could. Here is what I can remember him telling me plus a lot more of what my father told me that granddad had taught him.

## Foxes are very smart!

"Some animals are as clever as humans, so don't take them for granted!" Granddad respected all animals but said that the fox was the one that he learned a few tricks from. One day we were in a field where there were some sheep grazing. The field was fenced in barbed wire and all along the fence there were clumps of their wool caught in the wire. Out of the woods a fox was creeping along the fence. "Will he harm the sheep?" I asked. "No! Watch him." Granddad said.

As the fox went along the fence he started to pull some clumps of wool from the barbs, until he had quite a bunch, about the size of an apple, held in his teeth. "Why is he doing that?" I hardly got the question out when granddad said," Quiet! And watch." The fox went along the fence to a small pond at the edge of the field and stood there for about a minute. Then he walked into the pond until the water almost covered his back. He stayed there for another minute. Then he started to swim very slowly in circles, with just the tip of his nose showing above the water, and the clump of wool floating just in front of it. He then let go of the wool and it floated away from him and he swam to the shore, walked back along the fence and then went into the woods.

"Why did he do that, granddad?" I asked. Granddad laughed. "I told you they were clever. That fox used the sheep's wool to get rid of his fleas. When he walked into the pond and stopped the fleas all climbed up to the top of his back as that was the part of the fox that was out of the water. Then as he was swimming the fleas all jumped into the wool as that was dry. Then he let go of the wool and all the fleas floated away!"

My father told me the following stories about foxes. On a moonlit night, a fox would walk in circles beneath a tree where pheasants were roosting. As the fox went round and round the pheasants would follow him with their eyes. Soon at least one of the pheasants would become dizzy and fall off the branch onto the ground. The fox then had his next meal! Granddad used this knowledge to get pheasants at night, so quietly that the gamekeeper was never alerted. What granddad did was so simple. At night when there was no moon, he would stand under a tree where pheasants were roosting. He would light a cigarette, hold his arm out to full length and make a large circle with the cigarette glowing in the dark. The pheasants followed this light and soon one would fall down and suffer the same fate as those that had followed the fox's antics.

Another clever trick that a fox would use is to hide behind a tree close to a pond where ducks were swimming. Mr. Fox would very slowly poke his head around the tree so that the ducks could just see it, and then quickly hide again. Ducks are very curious and would start to swim towards the tree. The fox would do this again and again until a duck would climb onto dry land near the tree. Then the fox would go around the other side of the tree and creep up behind the duck and grab his dinner.

I am one of the few people alive who remember Sam Bourne and some of the stories about him that are part of the history of Mid-Sussex. Hopefully you enjoyed these stories and maybe have a different view of the poachers of the late 19th century and the early 20th century. Here is a photo of my Grandparents at the door of their home in Kents Road

# About the Author

**Ken Bourne is a third generation gardener and farmer. He was born in Sussex, England. He has extensive experience of working on the land, now purely organic. He has operated nurseries and garden centres in the UK, Abu Dhabi and for the last 35 years in Canada.**

**He writes extensively about the importance of the health of the soil. He is very concerned with the effects of climate change and the loss of arable land for food production.**

**His current nursery is in Forest Grove, British Columbia, Canada. Although he reached retiring age a decade ago he still operates the nursery, single handed, and writes about his love of gardening, horses, dogs and the history of the county of Sussex.**

**All authors rely on feedback to improve their writing. When you have finished reading this book would you please write an honest review and put it on Amazon.so that other potential purchasers can make a better decision.**

Printed in Great Britain
by Amazon

32831827R00036